Instant Pot Cookbook

Low Carb, Easy and Healthy Instant Pot Pressure Cooker Recipes That Taste Incredible

Brandon Hearn © 2018

Table of Contents

Introduction

The instant pot is a genius invention that will help you to save time in the kitchen without sacrificing home cooked, healthy meals. You can even tailor it to a specific diet, such as the low carb diet just like in this book. With the instant pot, you can kiss long cooking time goodbye, and the cleanup can be a breeze! In this book you'll learn about the instant pot and how to use it, benefits, and various low carb recipes to get you started. Remember that healthy eating doesn't have to be hard, and with the instant pot, your hours in the kitchen are at an end. there's no reason to slave over the stove for healthy meals.

An Instant Pot Guide

Before you get started on your instant pot journey, you'll want to get used to the instant pot and how to use it. Here is a guide to instant pot buttons and settings that will help you to get started with the recipes in this book.

Manual/Pressure Cook
When you use this button it automatically sets it for high pressure. You can change the cook time by using the plus and minus button. Of course, you'll hear a beep when your pressure cooker starts.

Sauté
This helps you to brown meat, cook vegetables, and simmer ingredients. You'll use this a lot to add texture to your meal and help to thicken sauces.
Keep Warm/Cancel
This helps you to cancel whatever you had going, and it'll keep your food warm until you're ready to serve it.

Soup/Broth
This button cooks on high pressure for a half hour. You will sometimes need to adjust the time.

Meat/Stew
This button will cook on high pressure for thirty-five minutes, but you can adjust the pre time.

Rice
You probably won't be using this button on a low arb diet, but it cooks on low pressure. It's completely automatic, so there's no need to do anything else.

Poultry
This will automatically set it to high pressure for fifteen minutes. You can adjust to cook for as little as five minutes.

Bean/Chili

This will cook at high pressure for a half hour, but it can go as low as twenty-five minutes.

Porridge

This will cook at high pressure for fifteen minutes. It can be adjusted as high as thirty minutes or as low as five minutes.

Multigrain

This will cook at high pressure for forty minutes, but it only can be adjusted up to forty-five minutes. It can go as low as twenty minutes in most models.

Steam

This is great for vegetables, and it cooks at high pressure for ten minutes. Some models will cook at fifteen minutes. You can usually steam something for as little as three minutes. To use this function, you'll have to add in a rack or steamer basket and place the water underneath it.

Delay Start

Not every instant pot will actually have this setting, but it allows you to set how long you want the instant pot to wait until it starts cooking.

Instant Pot Benefits

There are many benefits to using the instant pot, so in this chapter we're going to go through all of the ways the instant pot will make your life easier.

Slow Cooking & Pressure Cooking

You probably grew up with slow cooked meals, but you can now throw out that old slow cooker. Instead, the instant pot will make savory dishes in the same way, so you don't even need to change out your old recipes. Of course, it's also a pressure cooker too, which means that you can cut out half of the cooking time compared to traditional recipes. If you're on a tight schedule, then the instant pot can help to save you time by cooking quickly or just putting everything on and going about your day like you would with a crockpot.

You Can Make Desserts!

You don't need to bake to get delicious desserts anymore. You can make pudding, cheesecake, and so much more in the instant pot. So, there's no reason not to satisfy your sweet tooth. So once again, the instant pot comes in handy for any time of the day.

It's Safe

There are numerous onboard safety features for this kitchen gadget, so you don't have to worry about it being unsafe. Despite it using pressure to cook, as long as you follow the guidelines that you'll learn about in your manual, there is no worry. There are sensors that detect if the lid is locked, and it won't even take on prepare unless the cover is clamped down tight. When you factor in the pre-programmed settings, its safe and easy to use.

Clean Up is a Breeze

The easy clean up is one of the instant pot's greatest benefits. Its easy to clean because everything is just one pot. There's no need to clean up ten to twelve dishes. You don't need any fancy tools, and most of the parts are completely dishwasher safe. Not only will you be saving cooking time with the instant pot, but you save cleanup time as well.

Breakfast Recipes

Start your day off low carb with these simple breakfast recipes.

Scotch Eggs

Serves: 4 **Time:** 30 Minutes
Calories: 288 **Protein:** 27 Grams
Fat: 16 Grams **Carbs:** 1 Gram
Ingredients:

- 4 Eggs
- 1 lb. Ground Sausage
- 1 Tablespoon Vegetable Oil

Directions:

1. Start by placing your trivet in the instant pot, pouring in a cup of water. Add your eggs onto the trivet, and cook on high pressure for ten minutes.
2. use a quick release, and peel your eggs.
3. Wrap your eggs in the sausage, and then remove your rack from the instant pot. Drain your pot, and then press sauté, adding in your oil.
4. Sauté your eggs in the oil before placing them to the side.
5. Add your trivet back in, and then add in a cup of water. Place your eggs on the trivet, and cook for six minutes. Use a quick release, and serve warm.

Omelet Quiche

Serves: 4 **Time:** 10 Minutes
Calories: 365 **Protein:** 29 Grams
Fat: 24 Grams **Carbs:** 6 Grams
Ingredients:
- ½ Cup Half & Half
- 6 Eggs, Beaten
- 8 Ounces Canadian Bacon, Chopped
- Sea Salt & Black Pepper to Taste
- ¾ Cup Bell Pepper, Diced
- 4 Spring Onions, Sliced Thin
- ¾ Cup Cheddar Cheese, Shredded

Directions:
1. Get out a souffle dish, and then grease it with cooking spray.
2. Pour in one and a half cups of water into your instant pot before adding in your trivet.
3. Get out a bowl, and whisk your eggs with milk. Season with salt and pepper.
4. take your souffle dish and spread your bacon, peppers and cheese into it before pouring in your egg mixture. Mix well, and then top with foil.
5. Place your souffle dish onto the trivet, and then cook on high pressure for ten minutes. Use a quick release, and then remove the foil. Garnish with green onions and serve warm.

Stuffed Bell Pepper

Serves: 2 **Time:** 5 Minutes
Calories: 301 **Protein:** 0.7 Grams
Fat: 31.3 Grams **Carbs:** 4.2 Grams
Ingredients:

- 2 Slices Whole Wheat Bread, Toasted
- 2 Slices Smoked Gouda
- 2 Eggs, Chilled
- 1 Small Bunch Arugula
- 2 Bell Peppers, Deseeded

Hollandaise Sauce:

- 2/3 Cup Mayonnaise, Reduced Fat
- ½ Teaspoon Sea Salt, Fine
- 1 Tablespoon White Wine Vinegar
- 1 Teaspoon Lemon Juice, Fresh
- 1 Teaspoon Turmeric
- 1 ½ Teaspoons Dijon mustard
- 3 Tablespoons Orange Juice

Directions:

1. Mix all of your sauce ingredients in a bowl, whisking until well combined. Cover in plastic wrap, and place your sauce in the fridge until you're ready to use it.

2. Crack an egg into each bell pepper, and then wrap it in foil.

3. Add a cup of water into your instant pot before adding in your trivet. Place your bell peppers on the trivet.

4. Seal your instant pot, and then cook on low pressure for four minutes. Use a quick release, and then remove your pepper cups, slicing each one in half.

5. Stack toast, a slice of cheese, and a half a cup, and then drizzle with sauce before serving.

Egg Cups

Serves: 4 **Time:** 25 Minutes
Calories: 239 **Protein:** 15 Grams
Fat: 17 Grams **Carbs:** 5 Grams
Ingredients:

- 4 Eggs
- Butter, Unsalted
- 1 Cup Vegetables, Diced (Mushrooms, Tomatoes, Bell Pepper & Onion)
- ½ Cup Sharp Cheddar Cheese, Grated
- ¼ Cup Half & Half
- 1 Teaspoon Sea Salt, Fine
- 1 Teaspoon Black Pepper, Ground
- 2 Tablespoons Cilantro, Fresh & Chopped
- ½ Cup Cheese, Shredded for Garnish

Directions:

1. Grease four jars with butter, and then get out a bowl. Beat your eggs, and then add in your salt pepper, half-and-half, cheese and vegetables. Make sure to add in your cilantro, and mix well. Divide between your four half pint jars. Wide mouth jars will be easiest, and they need to b heatproof glass.

2. place your lids on your jars, but do not tighten them. This will help to keep water out of your eggs.

3. pour two cups of water into your cooking pot, and then add in your trivet. Put your jars onto the trivet, and lock the lid. Cook on high pressure for five minutes, and then use a quick release. Remove the lids from the jars, and then top with the cheese of your choice before serving.

4. Put your eggs under a broiler for two to three minutes to melt your cheese before serving.

Easy Frittata

Serves: 3
Time: 15 Minutes
Calories: 237
Protein: 15.6 Grams
Fat: 17.8 Grams
Carbs: 2.9 Grams

Ingredients:
- ¼ Teaspoon sea Salt, Fine
- ¼ Cup Cheddar Cheese, Shredded
- ¼ Teaspoon White Pepper
- ½ Cup Green Bell Pepper, Chopped
- 1 ½ Teaspoons Heavy Cream
- 1 Cup Italian Sausage, Cooked
- 4 Eggs
- ½ Teaspoon Italian Seasoning

Directions:

1. Get out a seven-inch round pan, and spray it down with cooking spray or use olive oil. Pour one and a half cups of water into your instant pot, and then place your trivet in it.

2. Get out a bowl, and whisk your Italian seasoning, heavy cream, eggs, salt and white pepper together.

3. In your pan layer your bell pepper, sausage, and cheese.

4. Pour the egg mixture over it, and then cover your pan using tin foil.

5. Place them in the trivet, and then cook on high pressure for fifteen minutes. Use a quick release and serve warm.

Smoked Salmon with Eggs

Serves: 4 **Time:** 5 Minutes
Calories: 241 **Protein:** 17.5 Grams
Fat: 18.3 Grams **Carbs:** 0.9 Grams
Ingredients:
- 4 Slices Smoked Salmon
- 4 Eggs
- 4 Slices Cheddar Cheese
- 4 Basil Leaves for Garnish
- Olive Oil as Needed

Directions:
1. Add a c up of water into your instant pot before adding in your trivet.

2. Get to ramekins, greasing them with olive oil. Crack an egg into each, and then add in a slice of cheese, topping with smoked salmon and a basil leave. Cover each one with foil, and cook on high pressure for four minutes.

3. Use a quick release and serve warm.

Egg Casserole

Serves: 4 **Time:** 22 Minutes
Calories: 343**Protein:** 20 Grams
Fat: 23 Grams **Carbs:** 12 Grams
Ingredients:

- 8 Eggs
- ½ Cup Bell Pepper, Diced
- ½ Cup Sausage, Diced
- Sea Salt & Black Pepper to Taste
- ½ Cup Onion, Diced
- ¼ Cup Whole Milk
- ¾ Cup Cheddar Cheese
- ¼ Teaspoon Garlic Salt

Directions:

1. Start by getting out a pan that fits into your instant pot and grease it. Pour in a cup and a half of water, and then add in your trivet.
2. in your dish, spread out your bell pepper, onion, cheese and sausage.
3. Whisk your eggs with salt and pepper, and then stir in your milk. Pour this over your sausage mixture, and then cover it in foil. Place the dish on the trivet.

4. Seal the lid, and then cook on high pressure for twelve minutes. Allow for a natural pressure release for ten minutes before using a quick release for the remaining pressure. Serve warm.

Broccoli Frittata

Serves: 4 **Time:** 45 Minutes
Calories: 372 **Protein:** 21.2 Grams
Fat: 29.4 Grams **Carbs:** 6.1 Grams

Ingredients:
- 1 Yellow Onion, Small & Diced
- 2 Tablespoons Butter
- 4 Cloves Garlic, Minced
- 1 Cup Broccoli Florets, Chopped
- 4 Eggs
- ¼ Cup Coconut Milk
- 1 Teaspoon Sea Salt
- 1 Lemon, Zested
- 1 Tablespoon Italian Parsley, Fresh & Chopped
- 1 Teaspoon Thyme, Fresh & Chopped
- 1 ½ Cups Cheddar Cheese, Shredded
- 6-8 Slices Turkey Bacon, Cooked & Crumbled
- 1 Cup Water

Directions:

1. Throw your oil into your instant pot, and then press sauté. Once it's hot, add in your onions and garlic. Cook for about seven minutes or until your onion caramelizes. Add in your broccoli, cooking for another four minutes.

2. Get outa heatproof dish, and then grease it. Whisk your eggs and milk together before adding in your parsley, lemon zest, thyme and salt. Stir in your broccoli, cheddar and bacon. Pour it into the dish, and cover with foil. Put your dish on the trivet, with a cup of water in your instant pot. Cook on high pressure for twenty-three minutes.

3. Use a natural pressure release for ten minutes before using a quick release for any remaining pressure.

Ham & Spinach Frittata

Serves: 8 **Time:** 5 Hours
Calories: 152 **Protein:** 11 Grams
Fat: 11 Grams **Carbs:** 3 Grams

Ingredients:
- 8 Eggs, Beaten
- 2 Cloves Garlic
- ½ Cup Coconut Milk, Canned
- 1 Onion, Small & Chopped
- 2 Cups Spinach, Fresh & Chopped
- 1 Cup Ham, Diced
- 1 Teaspoon Coconut Oil
- Sea Salt & Black Pepper to Taste

Directions:
1. PRs sauté, and then add in your coconut oil. Once it's hot, add in your onion and garlic. Sauté for five minutes before adding in your ham. Season with salt and pepper before adding in your eggs and coconut milk.
2. Add in your spinach and stir well. Sauté for a minute, and then press slow cook, setting it for five hours. Serve warm.

No Crust Quiche

Serves: 4
Time: 40 Minutes **Calories:** 460
Protein: 29.5 Grams **Fat:** 33.4 Grams **Carbs:** 10 Grams

Ingredients:
- 6 Eggs, Beaten
- ½ Cup Whole Milk
- Sea Salt & Black Pepper to Taste
- 1 Cup Ground Sausage, Cooked
- 4 Slices Bacon, Cooked & Crumbled
- 2 Green Onions, Chopped
- 1 Cup Cheddar Cheese, Shredded
- ½ Cup Ham, Diced

Directions:
1. Get out a souffle dish, and then add a cup of water into your instant pot. Place your trivet into the instant pot, and then get out a bowl. Whisk your salt, pepper, milk and eggs.
2. Spread your bacon, sausage, ham, cheese and green onions in a souffle dish. Pour your egg mixture over it, and then secure it with foil. Put a trivet into your instant pot, and then add in your dish. Cook on high pressure for thirty minutes. Use a natural pressure release for ten minutes before using a quick release on any remaining pressure. Serve warm.

Lunch Recipes

You don't have to blow your carb or calorie count on lunch. Try these easy recipes instead.

Pork Carnitas

Serves: 12 **Time:** 1 Hour 30 Minutes
Calories: 190 **Protein:** 11.8 Grams
Fat: 14.5 Grams **Carbs:** 2.4 Grams

Ingredients:
- 1 ½ Tablespoons Sea Salt, Fine
- 1 Tablespoon Oregano
- 2 Teaspoon Ground Cumin
- 1 Teaspoon Black Pepper
- 6 lbs. Pork Butt Roast
- ½ Teaspoon Chili Powder
- ½ Teaspoon Ground Paprika
- 2 Tablespoons Olive oil
- 1 cup Orange Juice

- 1 Onion, Chopped
- ¼ Cup Water
- 4 Cloves Garlic, Minced

Directions:

1. Season your pork butt with all seasoning, and then allow it to marinate for three hours. Pres sauté, and then add in your oil. Roast your pork for five minutes per side.

2. Add all of your remaining ingredients in, and then cook on high pressure for ninety minutes.

3. Use a quick release, and shred your meat before serving warm with sauce. You can serve on bread or over rice.

Easy Chili

Serves: 8 **Time:** 30 Minutes
Calories: 306 **Protein:** 23 Grams
Fat: 18 Grams **Carbs:** 13 Grams

Ingredients:
- 4 Ounces Chilies
- 2 lbs. Beef
- 1 Onion, Chopped
- 8 Tomatoes, Chopped
- 8 Cloves Garlic, Chopped
- 2 Tablespoons Worcestershire Sauce
- 2 Tablespoons Cumin
- ¼ Cup Chili Powder
- 1 Tablespoon Oregano
- 2 Tablespoons Sea Salt, Fine
- 1 Tablespoon Black Pepper
- 1 Bay Leaf

Directions:

1. Start by pressing sauté, and then add in your oil. Once your oil begins to shimmer, add in your onion. Cook until it becomes translucent, and then add in your garlic. Cook for another minute. It should become fragrant.

2. Place your ground beef in, and then sauté for another eight to ten minutes. Then throw in your remaining ingredients.

3. Cook on high pressure for thirty minutes, and then use a quick release. Serve warm.

Taco Soup

Serves: 6 **Time:** 30 Minutes
Calories: 403 **Protein:** 46 Grams
Fat: 18 Grams **Carbs:** 12 Grams

Ingredients:
- 1 ½ Tablespoons Coconut Oil
- 1 Yellow Onion
- 4 Bell Pepper
- 2 lbs. Ground Beef
- 2-3 Tablespoon Chili powder
- 4-6 Tablespoons Spices as Desired
- Sea Salt & Black Pepper to Taste
- 8 Tomatoes, Chopped
- 24 Ounces Bone Broth
- 5 Ounces Coconut Milk

Directions:

1. Press sauté, and then add in your oil. Once it's hot added in your onion and bell pepper.
2. Throw in your beef, and brown it. Strain any grease out before placing it back into the pot.
3. Throw in the remaining spices, and then add in your green chilies, broth, coconut milk and tomatoes.
4. Close the lid, and cook on high pressure for twenty-five minutes.
5. serve warm.

Seafood Gumbo

Serves: 8 **Time:** 20 Minutes
Calories: 346 **Protein:** 9 Grams
Fat: 12 Grams **Carbs:** 9 Grams

Ingredients:
- 2 Onion
- 3 Tablespoons Cajun Seasoning
- 3 Tablespoons Avocado Oil
- 24 Ounces Sea Bass Fillets
- 2 Bell Peppers
- 4 Celery Ribs
- 26 Ounces Tomatoes, Diced
- ¼ Cup Tomato Paste
- 3 Bay Leaves
- 2 lbs. Shrimp
- 1 ½ Cups Bone Broth

- Sea Salt & Black Pepper to Taste

Directions:

1. Season your sea bass with Cajun seasoning, salt and pepper, and make sure it's rubbed in.

2. Press sauté, and then add in your oil and sea bass chunks, and sauté for four minutes. Put your sea bass chunks to the side.

3. Add your pepper, celery and onion to your instant pot, cooking for two minutes before adding the fish back in. add in your bay leaf, bone broth, tomatoes and tomato paste. Stir well.

4. Cook for five minutes on high pressure, and then use a quick release before serving.

Broccoli Soup

Serves: 8 **Time:** 30 Minutes
Calories: 117 **Protein:** 3 Grams
Fat: 7 Grams **Carbs:** 11 Grams

Ingredients:
- 4 Cups Broccoli
- 6 Cloves Garlic
- 1 Leek, Chopped
- 1 Potato, Chopped
- 8 Cups Vegetable Broth
- Sea Salt & Black Pepper to Taste

Directions:
1. Throw all of your ingredients into your instant pot, and then close your lid. Cook on high pressure for five minutes.
2. Once your soup has cooled down some, use an immersion blender, blending until creamy. Serve warm.

Easy Ramen

Serves: 3
Time: 25 Minutes
Calories: 598 **Protein:** 76.6 Grams
Fat: 24 Grams **Carbs:** 11.3 Grams
Ingredients:

- 3 Chicken Breasts, boneless & Skinless
- 1 Cup Celery, chopped
- ½ Onion, Chopped
- 1 Cup Carrots, Chopped
- Sea Salt & Black Pepper to Taste
- ½ Teaspoon Thyme
- 1 Teaspoon Garlic
- 4 Cups Chicken Bone Broth
- 1 cup Water
- 3 Cups Ramen Noodles

Directions:

1. Start by throwing all of your ingredients except for your ramen noodles into your instant pot before closing the lid. Cook on high pressure for twenty minutes.
2. Use a quick release, and then press sauté. Stir in your noodles, allowing them to cook for five more minutes before serving warm.

Chicken Soup

Serves: 6 **Time:** 45 Minutes
Calories: 455 **Protein:** 29 Grams
Fat: 32 Grams **Carbs:** 12 Grams

Ingredients:
- 6 Chicken Thighs
- 2 Tablespoons Avocado Oil
- 1 Onion
- 3 Carrots, Chopped
- 3 Celery Ribs, Chopped
- 4 Cups Chicken Broth
- 2 Bay Leaves
- Sea Salt & Black Pepper to Taste
- 1 Teaspoon Parsley, Dried
- 2 Cloves Garlic, Minced
- 1 Teaspoon Thyme, Dried

Directions:

1. Press sauté, and then pour your olive oi into your instant pot. Once your oil begins to shimmer, add in your chicken thighs, browning on both sides. place your chicken to the side.

2. Add another teaspoon of oil, and then sauté your celery, onion and carrots. Cook for about two minutes.

3. Add remaining vegetables, and pour in your broth. Add all ingredients to the instant pot, and press soup mode.

4. Debone your chicken and shred it before serving your soup warm.

Cheddar & Broccoli Soup

Serves: 6
Time: 25 Minutes
Calories: 117
Protein: 3 Grams
Fat: 7 Grams
Carbs: 11 Grams

Ingredients:
- 2 Heads Broccoli, Chopped
- 4 Cups Chicken Broth
- 1 Cup Heavy Cream
- 2 Cups Cheddar Cheese
- Sea Salt & Black Pepper to Taste

Directions:
1. Put your broth and broccoli into your instant pot, and then cook on high pressure for three minutes.
2. Use a quick release, and then add your remaining ingredients. Use an immersion blender to puree until smooth before serving.

Snack Recipes

Low carbs and tasty snacks are possible! This chapter can teach you some easy low carb snack recipes.

Taco Dip

Serves: 6 **Time:** 35 Minutes
Calories: 385 **Protein:** 26 Grams
Fat: 26 Grams **Carbs:** 12 Grams

Ingredients:
- 5 Ounces Green Chilies, Canned & Diced
- 1 Cup Onion, Chopped
- 1 lb. Ground Beef, 80% Lean
- 10 Ounces Tomatoes with Chilies, Canned & Drained
- 3 Tablespoons Taco Seasoning
- 1 ½ Cups Sharp Cheddar Cheese, Grated
- 4 Cloves Garlic, Minced

Directions:

1. Press sauté, and then cook on high heat. Add in your onion, garlic and ground beef. You'll need to break up any clumps and brown your meat, which will take about two minutes.

2. stir in your chilies, tomatoes and taco seasoning before locking the lid. Cook on high pressure for five minutes. Allow for a natural pressure release for ten minutes, and then use a quick release to get rid of any remaining pressure. Add in your cheese before stirring. Serve warm.

Cream of Celery Soup

Serves: 4 **Time:** 20 Minutes
Calories: 174 **Protein:** 2.8 Grams
Fat: 14.6 Grams **Carbs:** 10.5 Grams
Ingredients:

- 1 Cup Coconut milk
- 1 Onion, Chopped
- 6 Cups Celery, Chopped
- 2 Cups water
- ½ Teaspoon Dill
- Sea Salt to Taste

Directions:

1. Throw all of your ingredient into your instant pot, and cook on high pressure for twenty minutes.

2. Use a quick release, and then use an immersion blender to blend until smooth. Serve warm.

Vanilla Jell-O

Serves: 6
Time: 6 Minutes **Calories:** 105
Protein: 3.3 Grams **Fat:** 7.9 Grams
Carbs: 5.2 Grams

Ingredients:
- 3 Tablespoons Erythritol
- 1 Cup Boiling Water
- 2 tablespoons Gelatin Powder, Unsweetened
- 1 Cup Heavy Cream
- 1 Teaspoon Vanilla Extract, Pure

Directions:
1. Start by adding in your boiling water and then press sauté. Allow it to simmer.
2. Add in your gelatin, and mix until it dissolves.
3. Mix in the rest of your ingredients, pouring the mixture into Jell-O molds. Allow it to set in the fridge for two hours.

Cherry Compote

Serves: 8
Time: 10 Minutes
Calories: 46
Protein: 0 Grams
Fat: 0 Grams
Carbs: 12 Grams
Ingredients:

- ¼ Teaspoon Almond Extract
- 2 Tablespoons Lemon Juice, Fresh
- ¾ Cup Sugar
- 2 Tablespoons Water
- 2 Tablespoons Cornstarch

Directions:

1. Start by placing your lemon juice, cherries, and sugar in your instant pot, making sure it's mixed well. Close your lid, and choose steam, adjusting the time to five minutes. Allow for a natural pressure release.

2. Mix your cornstarch, water and almond extract together, and then pour in this slurry. Press sauté, and cook until the sauce thickens.

Chickpea Hummus

Serves: 8 **Time:** 20 Minute
Calories: 110 **Protein:** 4.1 Grams
Fat: 3.8 Grams **Carbs:** 0.2 Grams

Ingredients:
- 1 Bay Leaf
- 2 Tablespoons Tahini
- 4 Cloves Garlic
- 1 Lemon, juiced
- 1 Cup Chickpeas
- 1/4 Teapsoon Cumin
- ½ Teaspoon Sea Salt, Fine
- Dash Olive Oil
- ½ Teaspoon Parsley
- Dash Paprika

Directions:

1. Start by adding six cups of water into your instant pot along with your chickpeas. Press the lentils button and adjust for eighteen minutes. Allow for a natural pressure release.

2. Transfer your chickpeas into a food processor, and then add in your remaining ingredients. Process until smooth, and serve drizzled with olive oil.

Southwest Dip

Serves; 8 **Time:** 15 Minutes
Calories: 222 **Protein:** 11.2 Grams
Fat: 14.2 Grams **Carbs:** 13 Grams

Ingredients:
- 2 Tablespoons Olive Oil
- 4 Strips Bacon, Chopped
- ½ White Onion, Diced
- 1 ½ Cups Corn, Frozen
- 1 Jalapeno Pepper, Deseeded & Chopped
- 1 Clove Garlic, Minced
- 14 Ounces Tomatoes, Canned & Diced
- 4 Ounces Green Chilies, Canned & Diced
- 2 Teaspoons Chili Powder
- ½ Teaspoon Sea Salt, Fine
- 1 Teaspoon Cumin
- 8 Ounces Cream Cheese, Softened
- 1 Cup Cheddar cheese, Shredded
- 3 Tablespoons Cilantro, Fresh for Garnish

Directions:

1. Start by pressing sauté on your instant pot, and then cook your bacon for seven minutes. It should be crisp, and then put them aside.

2. Add in your corn, onion and jalapeno, cooking for another five minutes. Add in your garlic, cooking for a minute more.

3. Stir in your cumin, salt and chili powder, mixing well. Once it's mixed, add in your green chili, tomatoes and cream cheese, making sure it's well combined.

4. Close the lid, and cook on high pressure for five minutes before using a quick release. Stir before serving.

Buffalo Dip

Serves; 15 **Time:** 20 Minutes
Calories; 270 **Protein:** 20.6 Grams
Fat: 18 Grams **Carbs:** 6.1 Grams

Ingredients:
- 2 Chicken Breasts
- 16 Ounces Cream Cheese
- 1 Cup Ranch dressing
- ¾ Cup Hot Sauce
- 2 Green Onions, Chopped
- 3 Tablespoons Butter
- 2 Cups Cheddar Cheese, Shredded
- Crackers as Needed

Directions:
1. Start by mixing your butter, cream cheese, chicken, ranch and hot sauce before adding it into your instant pot. Close the lid, cooking on high pressure for twenty minutes before using a quick release.
2. Remove your chicken, and then mix in your cheese. Shred your chicken before adding it back in, mixing well before serving.

Ranch Dip

Serves: 8 **Time:** 5 Minutes
Calories: 258 **Protein:** 3.4 Grams
Fat: 27.1 Grams **Carbs:** 1.2 Grams
Ingredients:
- 1 Cup Egg White, beaten
- 1 Lemon, Juiced
- Sea Salt & Black Pepper to Taste
- 1 Cup Olive Oil
- 1 Teaspoon Mustard Paste

Directions:
1. Start by placing all of your instant pot, and make sure to whisk well. PRs sauté, cooking for two minutes. Do not stir!
2. Refrigerate it before serving.

Garlic Meatballs

Serves: 4
Time: 45 Minutes
Calories: 192 **Protein:** 32 Grams
Fat: 11 Grams **Carbs:** 3 Grams
Ingredients:

- 1 lb. Ground Beef
- 1 Cup Spinach, Fresh
- ¼ Cup Garlic
- Sea Salt & Black Pepper to Taste
- 4 Carrots, Large
- Bone Broth as Needed

Directions:

1. Chop your carrot into half inch chunks, and then add them with some bone broth into your instant pot.

2. mix your beef, garlic, salt and pepper together, and then add in your spinach. Roll them into meatball size, and arrange them on your carrot.

3. Cook for twenty minutes using high pressure, and then use a quick release before serving.

Buffalo Wings

Serves: 4 **Time:** 20 Minutes
Calories: 140 **Protein:** 25 Grams
Fat: 0.1 Grams **Carbs:** 5.1 Grams

Ingredients:
- 4 Chicken Breasts, Boneless & Skinless
- 2 Tablespoons Honey, Raw
- 4 Tablespoons Butter, Unsalted
- ½ Bottle Buffalo Wing Sauce of Your Choice
- 2 Tablespoons Tabasco Sauce

Directions:
1. Throw all of your ingredients into the instant pot, and then cook on high pressure for ten minutes.
2. Get out two forks to shred your chicken, and then add them back into your instant pot.
3. Press sauté, and then cook for five more minutes.

Dinner Recipes

One of the hardest things about the low carb diet is trying to find a filling dinner that delights the taste buds. That's where this chapter comes in handy!

Corned Beef

Serves: 6 **Time:** 55 Minutes
Calories: 228 **Protein:** 16 Grams
Fat: 16 Grams **Carbs:** 3 Grams

Ingredients:
- 2 ½ lbs. Corned Beef Brisket
- 20 Red Potatoes
- 4 Cups Beef Broth
- 2 Tablespoon Cornstarch
- 1 Spice Packet
- 1 Head cabbage
- 7 Garlic Cloves
- 1 Onion

Directions:

1. Put your potatoes, garlic, onion, and broth into your instant pot, and then sprinkle your spices over it.

2. close the lid, and cook for forty minutes using low pressure.

3. Shred your cabbage, and cook for another ten minutes.

4. Remove the meat, but make sure to leave the drippings in. make sure that all of your vegetables are out as well.

5. Blend your broth with your corn starch to create a slurry. Lower your temperature and continue to cook until it thickens.

6. Serve your beef drizzled with the sauce.

Adobo Chicken

Serves: 6 **Time:** 30 Minutes
Calories: 520 **Protein:** 25 Grams
Fat: 27 Grams **Carbs:** 17 Grams

Ingredients:
- 2 lbs. Chicken, Boneless
- 1 Tablespoon Turmeric
- 1 Tablespoon Garlic
- 4 Tomatoes, Chopped
- 7 Ounces Green Chilies
- ½ Cup Water

Directions:
1. Start by putting your chicken into your instant pot and then seasoning it. Add in your chilies and tomatoes.

2. pour your water in, and then cook for twenty-five minutes before using a quick release.

3. serve on its own or over rice.

Easy Pot Roast

Serves: 8 **Time:** 1 Hour 20 Minutes
Calories: 240 **Protein:** 25 Grams
Fat: 19 Grams **Carbs:** 2 Grams

Ingredients:
- 1 Cup Beef Broth
- 1 Onion, Chopped
- 1 Tablespoon Vegetable Oil
- 2 Bay leaves
- Lemon Pepper to Taste
- 3 lbs. Beef Chunk

Directions:
1. Rub your beef chunks down with lemon pepper, and then place it to the side.
2. Add your oil to your instant pot, and then press sauté. Once your oil has heated, then add in your meat. Brown it on both sides, and then remove the meat from the pot.
3. Add in your water, bay leaf and onion, placing your meat on top of the onion.

4. Cook on high pressure for seventy minutes, and then remove the lid. Cook more if you'd like your sauce to thicken more, but to do this press sauté, and allow it to thicken with time.

Pork Adobo

Serves: 6 **Time:** 30 Minutes
Calories: 342 **Protein:** 32 Grams
Fat: 19 Grams **Carbs:** 2 Grams
Ingredients:
- ½ Cup Soy Sauce
- 6 Cloves Garlic
- 2 lbs. Short Ribs
- 1 Cup Vinegar
- 1 Tablespoon Peppercorn
- 4 Bay Leaves
- ¼ Cup Brown Sugar
- 1 Tablespoon Cornstarch
- Sea Salt & Black Pepper to Taste

Directions:
1. Sauté your meat with garlic and oil, and then season with salt and pepper.
2. Add in your brown sugar, and blend, and then add in your remaining ingredients all except for your cornstarch.
3. cook for fifteen minutes on high pressure, and then use a quick release. Sauté, and then add in a water and cornstarch mixture. Bring it to a boil, and cook for five minutes.

Tomato & Feta Shrimp

Serves: 6 **Time:** 25 Minutes
Calories: 361 **Protein:** 30 Grams
Fat: 22 Grams **Carbs:** 13 Grams

Ingredients:
- 1 ½ Cups Onion, Chopped
- ½ Teaspoon Red Pepper Flakes
- 1 Tablespoon Garlic
- 3 Tablespoon Butter, Unsalted
- 14.5 Ounces Tomatoes, Canned, Diced & Undrained
- 1 Teaspoon Oregano
- 1 Teaspoon Sea Salt, Fine
- 1 Cup Feta Cheese, Crumbled
- ½ Cup Black Olives, Sliced
- ¼ Cup Parsley, Chopped
- 1 lb. Shrimp, Frozen & Peeled

Directions:

1. Start by pressing sauté, and then add in your butter. Once your butter begins to foam add in your red pepper flakes and garlic, cooking for a minute. They should become fragrant.

2. Add in your oregano, tomatoes, salt, and onion. Stir well, and then add in your frozen shrimp.

3. Lock your lid, and then cook on low pressure for one minute. Use a quick release, and then add in your tomato broth.

4. allow this mixture to cool slightly, and then sprinkle with olives, feta cheese and parsley. You can serve this warm on its own or over mashed cauliflower.

Sesame Chicken

Serves: 6 **Time:** 10 Minutes
Calories: 260 **Protein:** 36 Grams
Fat: 2 Grams **Carbs:** 10 Grams
Ingredients:

- 1 ½ lbs. Chicken Breasts, Skinless & Boneless
- 1 Tablespoon Garlic, Minced
- ¼ Cup Honey, Raw
- ¼ Cup Tamari
- 1 Teaspoon Red Pepper
- 2 Tablespoons Cornstarch
- 1 Tablespoon Sesame Seeds

Directions:

1. Start by pressing sauté, and add in some olive oil.

2. Place half of your chicken in, and sauté on both sides. do the second half in a different batch, making sure to brown it on both sides.

3. get out a mixing bowl, and mix all of your sauce ingredients together.

4. Place your chicken in the cooker, adding in your sauce. Cover your chicken, and then close the lid. Cook for four minutes, and then use a natural pressure release before serving.

Chili Lime Thighs

Serves: 5 **Time:** 45 Minutes
Calories: 120 **Protein:** 15 Grams
Fat: 3 Grams **Carbs:** 7 Grams

Ingredients:
- 4 Chicken Thighs
- 2 Tablespoons Olive Oil
- 3 Cloves Garlic, Minced
- 1 Teaspoon Cumin
- 1 Tablespoon Chili Powder
- ½ Cup Chicken Stock
- ¼ Cup Cilantro, Fresh & Chopped
- 1 Tablespoon Arrowroot powder
-

Directions:

1. Start by mixing your chili powder, garlic, lime juice, olive oil and cumin together in a bowl.

2. rub your chicken down with the mixture, and allow it to sit for a half hour.

3. Press sauté and add in a tablespoon of olive oil. Once it's heated, add in your chicken thighs, sautéing on both sides.

4. Add in your stock, and click the poultry setting. Set your time to twelve minutes. While this cook, get out a cup and mix your arrowroot powder and two tablespoons of water together. Make sure it's mixed well to take a slurry.

5. Add your arrowroot mixture, and then cook for another eight to ten minutes. Your sauce should thicken, and then serve it immediately.

Roasted Chicken

Serves: 4 **Time:** 45 Minutes
Calories: 250 **Protein:** 30 Grams
Fat: 31 Grams **Carbs:** 1 Gram

Ingredients:
- 2 Tablespoons Rosemary, Fresh
- 1 Tablespoon Sea Salt, Fine
- ½ Tablespoon Black Pepper
- 1 Bay leaf
- 1 Tablespoon Thyme
- 1 tablespoon Olive Oil
- 1 Chicken, Whole
- 1 Tablespoon Lemon Juice, Fresh

Directions:
1. Pres sauté, and then add in your olive oil. Cook your chicken, browning on both sides before placing it to the side.
2. Add in your trivet, and then add in your lemon juice, rosemary, chicken stock, and thyme. Season with salt and pepper.
3. Press poultry, and close the lid. Cook for twenty-five to thirty minutes.
4. Allow to cool before serving. Remember to remove your bay leaf.

Salsa Chicken

Serves: 6 **Time:** 15 Minutes
Calories: 150 **Protein:** 26 Grams
Fat: 2 Grams **Carbs:** 5 Grams
Ingredients:
- ½ Teaspoon Chili
- 1 Tablespoon Paprika
- ½ Tablespoon Cumin
- 17 Ounces Salsa Verde
- 2 lbs. chicken Breasts, Boneless & Skinless
- 1 Tablespoon Black Pepper
- 1 Tablespoon sea Salt
- ½ Onion, Diced
- 1 Jalapeno, Diced
- ¼ Cup Cilantro, Fresh & Chopped
- 1 Lime, Fresh

Directions:
1. Place half of your salsa into the instant pot, and then season with salt and pepper. Add in your cilantro, jalapeno, and onion. Add in your chicken, and mix well.
2. Add in another ¼ cup of salsa, and then place your other ¼ cup to the side. Close your lid, and cook on high heat for ten minutes. Use a quick release, and then shred your chicken.

3. Place it back into your pot, and then add in your lime juice and salsa.

Baba Ghanoush

Serves: 4 **Time:** 40 Minutes
Calories: 96 **Protein:** 1 Gram
Fat: 9 Grams **Carbs:** 3 Grams
Ingredients:

- ¼ Teaspoon Liquid Smoke
- 1 Tablespoon Olive Oil
- 2 Tablespoons Parsley, Fresh & Chopped
- Pinch Smoked Paprika
- ½ Teaspoon Sea Salt, Fine
- 2 Tablespoons Tahini
- ¼ Cup Water
- 5 Cloves Garlic, Minced
- 6 Tablespoons Olive Oil, Divided
- 1 Eggplant, Peeled, Halved Crosswise, Sliced into Planks
- 2 Tablespoons Lemon Juice, Fresh

Directions:

1. Start by heating your instant pot by pressing sauté, and then add in two tablespoons of oil. Once it starts to shimmer, add in your eggplant slices, but do not stir them. You'll want to char the bottom. Place them to the side once

they're charred. Continue until all of your eggplant slices are done. This will take ten to fifteen minutes. Use a spatula to get the char form the bottom of the pot.

2. Throw in your water, slat and garlic and then add the charred eggplant again. Lock your lid, and cook on high pressure for three minutes. Use a quick release before unlocking the lid.

3. If there is still too much water, then sauté until the water cooks off.

4. Get out an immersing blender, and blend until smooth, adding in your lemon juice, liquid smoke and tahini.

5. Spoon into bowls before topping with olive oil and smoked paprika. It's great served with raw vegetables!

Citrus Herb Chicken

Serves: 4 **Time:** 5 Minutes
Calories: 250 **Protein:** 30 Grams
Fat: 31 Grams **Carbs:** 1 Gram

Ingredients:
- 3 Tablespoons Butter, Grass Fed
- 1 ½ Tablespoon Sea Salt, Fine
- 4 Chicken Thighs
- 5 Sprigs Thyme, Fresh
- 4 Cloves Garlic, Minced
- 1 Yellow Onion, Sliced
- ½ lb. Chorizo
- 1/3 Cup Tomatoes
- ½ Cup Green Olives, Pitted
- 1/3 Cup Orange Juice
- ¾ Cup Chicken Bone Broth
- Cilantro, Fresh to Garnish

Directions:

1. Press sauté on your pressure cooker, and then add in two tablespoons of olive oil. Add in your chicken thighs, and then sauté for five more minutes. Season with salt and pepper, and then place your chicken to the side.

2. Place your onion, garlic and thyme with a fat of your choice into the instant pot, and then sauté for five minutes. Add in your chorizo, and then add in your chicken.

3. add in your olives, bone broth, orange juice, and tomatoes. Cook for twenty minutes, and serve warm.

Italian Shredded Chicken

Serves: 8 **Time:** 15 Minutes
Calories: 170 **Protein:** 27 Grams
Fat: 7 Grams **Carbs:** 1 Gram

Ingredients:
- 1 Tablespoon Italian Seasoning
- 4 lbs. Chicken Breasts
- ½ Teaspoon Sea Salt, Fine
- ½ Teaspoon Ground Black Pepper
- 1 Cup Chicken Broth

Directions:
1. Place your chicken into the instant pot, and then add in your seasoning. Season well, and then pour your broth over your chicken.

2. Cook on high pressure for ten minutes, and then shred before serving with broth.

Zoodle Soup

Serves: 6 **Time:** 25 Minutes
Calories: 164 **Protein:** 19 Grams
Fat: 5 Grams **Carbs:** 10 Grams

Ingredients:
- 1 Tablespoon Olive oil
- 1 Onion, Diced
- 1 lb. Chicken Breasts, Boneless, Skinless & Sliced
- 2 Cloves Garlic, Minced
- 3 Carrots, Sliced
- 1 Bay leaf
- 6 Cups Chicken Broth
- 3 Stalks Celery, Sliced
- 1 Jalapeno Pepper, Diced
- 2 Tablespoons Apple Cider Vinegar
- 4 Zucchinis, Spiralized
- Sea Salt & Black Pepper to Taste

Directions:
1. Press sauté, and then add in your garlic and onion. Cook until it's fragrant, and then add in your celery, carrots, jalapeno and chicken breasts. Stir for a minute before seasoning with salt and pepper.
2. Add in your chicken broth, bay leaf, and apple cider vinegar. Close the lid, and cook on high pressure for twenty minutes before using a quick release.
3. Press sauté again, and then add in your zucchini, cooking for another three minutes. Serve warm.

Cabbage Soup

Serves: 6 **Time:** 35 Minutes
Calories: 428 **Protein:** 26.3 Grams
Fat: 24.8 Grams **Carbs:** 9.2 Grams

Ingredients:
- 1 Onion, Chopped
- 1 Tablespoon Avocado Oil
- 1 lb. Ground Beef
- ½ Teaspoon Garlic Powder
- 1 Can Tomatoes, diced
- Sea Salt & Black Pepper to Taste
- 6 Cups Bone Broth
- 1 lb. Cabbage, Shredded
- 2 Bay Leaves

Directions:
1. Press sauté, and then add in your oil. Once it heats up, sauté your beef and onions. Season with garlic, salt and pepper. Cook for two minutes, and then add in your bone broth, bay leaves, cabbage and iced tomatoes. Cook on high pressure for thirty minutes.
2. Use a quick release, and serve warm.

Mojo Chicken

Serves: 4 **Time:** 45 Minutes
Calories: 250 **Protein:** 30 Grams
Fat: 31 Grams **Carbs:** 1 Gram

Ingredients:
- 1 Tablespoon Lemon Juice, Fresh
- 1 Tablespoon Olive oil
- 1 Whole chicken
- 2 Tablespoons Rosemary, Fresh & Chopped
- 1 Tablespoon, Fresh & Chopped
- Sea Salt & Black Pepper to Taste
- 1 Bay Leaf

Directions:
1. Press sauté, and then add in your olive oil. Add in your chicken, and sauté on both sides. set it to the side, and then add in your trivet.
2. Throw in your chicken stock, lemon juice, rosemary and thyme. Season with salt and pepper, and then press your poultry button.
3. Cook for twenty-five to thirty minutes, and then remove the bay leaf before serving.

Side Dish Recipes

Now that you have some low carb main dishes, you'll need side dishes to go with it! These side dishes are tasty and won't raise your carb count too high.

Lemon Broccoli

Serves: 3 **Time:** 8 Minutes
Calories: 32 **Protein:** 1.8 Grams
Fat: 1.5 Grams **Carbs:** 4.1 Grams
Ingredients:
- 1 Head Broccoli, Chopped into Florets
- 1 Teaspoon Garlic Powder
- 1 Stick Butter, Melted
- 2 Tablespoons Lemon Juice, Fresh
- Sea Salt & Black Pepper to Taste

Directions:
1. Add your trivet into the instant pot before adding in a cup of water. Throw your florets into the trivet, and then cook on high pressure for eight minutes.
2. Use a quick release, and toss them into a bowl. Mix your remaining ingredients before serving.

Green Beans with Bacon

Serves: 6 **Time:** 30 Minutes
Calories: 165 **Protein:** 6 Grams
Fat: 13 Grams **Carbs:** 6 Grams
Ingredients:
- 6 Slices Bacon, Diced
- 1 Cup Onion, Diced
- ¼ Cup Water
- 4 Cups Green Beans, Halved
- Sea Salt & Black Pepper to Taste

Directions:
1. Start by pressing sauté, and then add in your onion and bacon. Cook for two to three minutes, and then add in your water, salt, pepper and green beans before locking your lid.
2. Cook on high pressure for four minutes before using a quick release. Season before serving if necessary.

Creamy Eggplant

Serves: 6 **Time:** 40 Minutes
Calories: 73 **Protein:** 1 Gram
Fat: 4 Grams **Carbs:** 6 Grams

Ingredients:
- 1 Onion, Small & Sliced Thin
- ½ Teaspoon Peanut Oil
- 1 Tomato, Chopped
- 4 Cups Eggplant, Chopped
- ¼ Teaspoon Cayenne
- ¼ Teaspoon Garam Masala
- ¼ Teaspoon Ground Turmeric
- ¼ Teaspoon Chaat Masala, Optional
- ¼ Teaspoon Sea Salt, Fine
- ¼ Cup Heavy Whipping Cream

Directions:

1. Add your oil in, and once it's heated add in your onion, tomato and eggplant. Your onion and tomato need to stay on the bottom so the dish cooks.

2. Do not stir. Sprinkle your seasoning, and still do not stir. Lock the lid, and cook on low pressure for four minutes, and then allow for a natural pressure

release for ten minutes. Once your ten minutes is up, then use a quick release for any remaining pressure.

3. Pres sauté, and then cook until it starts to bubble. Once it bubbles, add in the cream, and allow it to thicken. This should cook for about two more minutes to thicken properly. Serve warm.

Easy Baked Beans

Serves: 4 **Time:** 50 Minutes
Calories: 522 **Protein:** 26.5 Grams
Fat: 2.4 Grams **Carbs:** 10.2 Grams

Ingredients:
- 1 lb. Navy Beans, Dried
- 6 Cups Cold Water
- 6 Cloves Garlic, Chopped
- 1 Onion, Small & Diced
- 1 ¾ Cup Water, Cold
- ¼ Cup Maple Syrup
- ¼ Cup Blackstrap Molasses
- ¼ Teaspoon Sea Salt
- 2 Bay Leaves
- 2 Teaspoons Dijon Mustard
- 1 Teaspoons Apple Cider Vinegar

Directions:
1. Throw your beans and water into the instant pot, and then cook on high pressure for forty minutes. Allow for a quick release, and then strain your beans. Discard your water, and then add all of your ingredients back into the instant pot.
2. Cook for ten more minutes before serving.

Curried Carrots

Serves: 6 **Time:** 10 Minutes
Calories: 142 **Protein:** 4.3 Grams
Fat: 9.8 Grams **Carbs:** 12.1 Grams

Ingredients:
- 2 Carrots, Peeled 7 Julienned
- ¼ Cup Pumpkin Seeds, Roasted
- 1/3 Cup Tahini
- 1 Cup Raisins
- 2 Tablespoons Curry Powder
- 2 Tablespoons Maple Syrup
- ¼ Cup Lemon Juice
- ¼ Teaspoon Black Pepper

Directions:
1. Start by throwing all of your ingredients into the instant pot, and cook on high pressure for ten minutes. Allow for a natural pressure release.
2. Serve warm.

Brussel Sprouts

Serves: 4 **Time:** 20 Minutes
Calories: 67 **Protein:** 2 Grams
Fat: 5 Grams **Carbs:** 5.2 Grams

Ingredients:
- 1 lb. Brussel Sprouts
- 2 Tablespoons Olive Oil
- ¼ Cup Pine Nuts
- Sea Salt & Black Pepper to Taste

Directions:
1. Place your trivet in the instant pot, and then put in your steamer basket. Add a cup of water, and then put your Brussel sprouts in the basket.
2. Cook on high pressure for three minutes, and then use a quick release.
3. Season with salt, pepper, olive oil and pine nuts before serving.

Sweet Brussel Sprouts

Serves: 8 **Time:** 15 Minutes
Calories: 65 **Protein:** 0 Gram
Fat: 0 Grams **Carbs:** 3 Grams
Ingredients:

- 2 lbs. Brussel Sprouts
- ¼ Cup Orange Juice, Fresh
- 1 Teaspoon Orange Zest, Fresh
- 1 Tablespoon Butter
- 2 Tablespoons Maple Syrup
- Sea Salt & Black Pepper to Taste

Directions:

1. Throw all of your ingredients into your instant pot, and then cook for four minutes on high pressure. You'll need to make sure that your Brussel sprouts are at least cut in half first.
2. Use a quick release, and then stir your Brussel sprouts before serving.

Mango Mashed Potatoes

Serves: 6 **Time:** 12 Minutes
Calories: 142 **Protein:** 54 Grams
Fat: 1.9 Grams **Carbs:** 7 Grams

Ingredients:
- 1 Cup Milk
- ½ Stick Butter
- 2 lbs. Potatoes
- 1 Cup Water
- ½ Cup Mango Juice
- Sea Salt & Black Pepper to Taste

Directions:
1. Place your water, butter, and potatoes into the instant pot. Season with salt and pepper.
2. Secure your lid, and cook on high pressure for seven minutes.
3. Use a quick release, and then place your potatoes in a large mixing bowl. Mash your potatoes, and then add in your mango and milk. Make sure to mix well before serving.

Mushroom Loaded Green Beans

Serves: 5 **Time:** 30 Minutes
Calories: 120 **Protein:** 5 Grams
Fat: 5 Grams **Carbs:** 7 Grams

Ingredients:
- 1 lb. Green Beans
- 6 Ounces Bacon, Chopped
- ½ Onion, Sliced
- 8 Ounces Mushrooms, Sliced
- 1 Clove Garlic, Minced
- Splash Balsamic Vinegar
- Sea Salt & Black Pepper to Taste

Directions:
1. Pour a cup of water into your instant pot, and then add in your green beans.
2. close the lid, and cook for two minutes on high pressure.
3. Use a quick release, and then drain your green beans. Set your green beans to the side, and then press sauté.
4. Add your bacon and season with pepper. Mix well before adding in your mushrooms. Cook for a few more minutes, making sure that your bacon is crisp. You'll need to stir occasionally.
5. Add your green beans back, and add in your vinegar. Stir well before serving.

Easy Asparagus

Serves: 2
Time: 10 Minutes **Calories:** 26.8
Protein: 2.9 Grams
Fat: 0.19 Grams **Carbs:** 5.2 Grams

Ingredients:
- 2 Tablespoons Olive Oil
- 1 Tablespoon Onion Powder
- 1 Cup Water
- 1 lb. Asparagus
- Sea Salt & Black Pepper to Taste

Directions:
1. Place your water and steamer basket into the instant pot, and then put your asparagus into the instant pot.
2. sprinkle them with onion powder and olive oil.
3. Cook for three minutes on high pressure before using a quick release. Season with salt and pepper before serving.

Dessert Recipes

Desserts don't have to be hard, and they certainly don't have to be full of carbs. Enjoy these low carb dessert recipes.

Cocoa Macaroons

Serves: 15
Time: 10 Minutes
Calories: 141
Protein: 2.6 Grams
Fat: 15.2 Grams
Carbs: 8.1 Grams

Ingredients:
- 3 Cups Coconut Flakes
- 3 Eggs, Beaten
- 1/3 Cup Cocoa Powder
- ¼ Cup Coconut Oil
- 1 Tablespoon Liquid Stevia

Directions:

1. Press sauté, and then add all of your ingredients in, pouring in a quarter cup of water. Stir and cook for ten minutes.
2. Turn off your instant pot, and then scoop the mixture into small balls. Allow them to chill in the fridge for an hour before serving.

Blueberry & Lemon Cake

Serves: 2 **Time:** 10 Minutes

Calories: 259 **Protein:** 7.2 Grams

Fat: 20.9 Grams **Carbs:** 10.3 Grams

Ingredients:

- ½ Cup Coconut Milk
- 4 Eggs, large
- ½ Cup Coconut Flour
- 1 Teaspoon Baking Soda
- ½ Teaspoon Lemon Zest

Directions:

1. Place all of your ingredients in a bowl, and then pour it into a mug that is heatproof.
2. Add a cup of water to your instant pot before placing in your steam rack. Place your mug on top, and then cook on high pressure for ten minutes. Use a natural pressure release.

Brownie Batter Fudge

Serves: 10 **Time:** 6 Hours

Calories: 84 **Protein:** 1.5 Grams

Fat: 8.4 Grams **Carbs:** 1.2 Grams

Ingredients:

- ¾ Cup Coconut Milk
- 4 Egg Yolks, Beaten
- 2 Tablespoons Butter, Melted
- 5 Tablespoons Cacao Powder
- 1 Teaspoon Erythritol

Directions:

1. Place all of your ingredients into the instant pot, mixing well. Grease the inner pot, and then pour in your batter.
2. Slow cook for six hours.

Easy Cheesecake

Serves: 6 **Time:** 20 Minutes

Calories: 207 **Protein:** 5 Grams

Fat: 19 Grams **Carbs:** 4 Grams

Ingredients:

- 2 Teaspoons Lemon Juice, Fresh
- 2 Teaspoons Vanilla Extract, Pure
- ½ Cup Sour Cream, Room Temperature & Divided
- ½ Cup Swerve + 2 Teaspoons Swerve
- 8 Ounces Cream Cheese, Room Temperature
- 2 Eggs, Room Temperature

Directions:

1. Start by adding two cups of water into your instant pot, and then add in your trivet. Get out a six-inch spring form pan, lining it with parchment paper.

2. Take your food processor, and mix your vanilla, lemon juice, ¼ cup of your sour cream, cream cheese and a half a cup of swerve together. Blend until smooth, scraping the sides of your bowl as needed.

3. Add your eggs in, and blend for twenty to thirty more sections.

4. Pour your mixture into your pan, and then cover it with foil before placing it on your trivet. Cook on high pressure for twenty minutes, and then allow for a natural pressure release. While your pressure is releasing, mix your remaining ¼ cup of sour cream and two teaspoons of swerve to make a topping.

5. Allow your cheesecake to refrigerate for six to eight hours before topping and serving.

Creamy Mousse

Serves: 4 **Time:** 10 Minutes

Calories: 291 **Protein:** 3.5 Grams

Fat: 29.5 Grams **Carbs:** 9.2 Grams

Ingredients:

- 2 Cups Coconut Milk, Fresh
- 2 Teaspoons Vanilla Extract, Pure
- 2 Tablespoons Erythritol
- 2 Tablespoons Cocoa Powder, Sifted
- Cocoa Nibs for Garnish

Directions:

1. Start by placing all of your ingredients except for the cacao nibs, and then sauté for ten minutes.
2. Pour the mixture into ramekins, and allow it to cool in the fridge for an hour. Garnish with cocoa nibs before serving.

Apple Crisp

Serves: 4 **Time:** 12 Minutes

Calories: 200 **Protein:** 3 Grams

Fat: 14 Grams **Carbs:** 12 Grams

Ingredients:

- 2 Tablespoons Cinnamon
- ½ Tablespoon Nutmeg
- ½ cup Water
- 5 Apples
- 4 Tablespoons Butter
- 1 Tablespoons Maple Syrup
- ½ Cup Old Fashioned Oats
- ¼ Cup Flour
- ½ Teaspoon Sea Salt
- ¼ Cup Brown Sugar

Directions:

1. Put your apples in the instant pot, sprinkling them with nutmeg and cinnamon before pouring in your water and maple syrup.
2. get out a microwave safe bowl, and then melt your butter. Place your melted butter in the mixing bowl, adding in your slat, flour, oats and brown sugar. Mix well, and drop it in spoonsful over the apples.

3. Close your instant pot, and then cook for eight minutes on high pressure. Use a quick release, and serve with vanilla ice cream if desired.

Macadamia Brownies

Serves: 9 **Time:** 10 Minutes

Calories: 189 **Protein:** 1.9 Grams

Fat: 20 Grams **Carbs:** 3.3 Grams

Ingredients:

- 1 ½ Teaspoons Baking Powder
- 1 Teaspoon Vanilla Extract, Pure
- 1 Teaspoon Instant coffee
- 2 Eggs, Large
- ¾ Cup Macadamia Nuts
- ¾ Cup Erythritol
- ¾ Cup Almond Flour
- ¼ Cup Coconut Oil
- 5 Tablespoons Butter, Salted
- 3 Tablespoons Cocoa Powder

Directions:

1. Start by getting out a bowl and cream your butter. Add in your coconut oil and erythritol. Mix well before adding in your vanilla and eggs. It should be fully incorporated.

2. Add in your cocoa powder and coffee, mixing until well combined.

3. Add in your baking powder and almond flour, making sure it's mixed well.

4. Get out a spatula, and then fold in your macadamia nuts, and then get out a heat proof dish. Pour your batter into the dish, and then set it inside of your instant pot, and then spread it out evenly. Cover with foil, and then add a cup of water to your instant pot. Add in your steamer basket, and then place your dish in. press your steam button, and allow it to go through its full cycle. Allow it to cool slightly before serving, and only use a natural pressure release.

Key Lime Pie

Serves: 8 **Time:** 15 Minutes

Calories: 93 **Protein:** 1.9 Grams

Fat: 7.74 Grams **Carbs:** 4.67 Grams

Ingredients:

- 1/3 Cup Sour Cream
- ½ Cup Key Lime Juice
- 4 Egg Yolks, Large
- 1 Can Condensed Milk
- 1 Tablespoon Sugar
- ¾ Cup Graham Cracker Crumbs
- 3 Tablespoons Butter, Melted
- 2 Tablespoons Key Lime Zest

Directions:

1. Place a cup and a half of water into your instant pot before adding in your steamer rack, and then get out a spring form pan. Coat it with cooking spray, and then get out a bowl.

2. In your bowl mix your butter, sugar and graham crackers. Press to the bottom of your pan and place it in the fridge. This forms your crust.

3. Get out another bowl, and then beat your egg yolks until they turn a light yell, and then slowly add in your condensed milk.

4. Beat in your lime juice before adding in your zest and sour cream, mixing well.

5. Pour the batter into your pan, and then cover it with foil. Close the lid, and press team. Cook for fifteen minutes, and then use a natural pressure release.

6. Allow it to cool in the fridge before serving.

Pumpkin Pie Pudding

Serves: 6 **Time:** 40 Minutes

Calories: 188 **Protein:** 4 Grams

Fat: 17 Grams **Carbs:** 8 Grams

Ingredients:

- 2 Eggs
- ½ Cup Heavy Whipping Cream
- ¾ Cup Swerve
- 15 Ounces Pumpkin Puree, Canned
- 1 Teaspoon Pumpkin Pie Spice
- 1 Teaspoon Vanilla Extract
- ½ Cup Heavy Whipping Cream for Topping

Directions:

1. Start by greasing a six by three-inch pan, making sure that it's greased well.
2. Whisk your eggs in a bowl, and add in your remaining ingredients. Make sure that it's well combined.

3. Pour your mixture into your pan, and then cover with foil.

4. Pour two cups of water into your instant pot before adding in your trivet with your pan on top. Lock the lid, and then cook on high pressure for twenty minutes. Allow for a natural pressure release for ten minutes before using a quick release to get rid of any remaining pressure.

5. Allow it to cool in the fridge before serving. You should let it chill for six to eight hours for the best results.

Thai Coconut Custard

Serves: 4 **Time:** 1 Hour 5 Minutes

Calories: 202 **Protein:** 6 Grams

Fat: 18 Grams **Carbs:** 4 Grams

Ingredients:

- 1 Cup Coconut Milk
- 3 Eggs
- 1/3 Cup Swerve
- 3-4 Drops Vanilla Extract, Pure

Directions:

1. Start by greasing a six-inch bowl, and then set it to the side. This bowl should be heatproof so that it can go into your instant pot.
2. Get out a different bowl and whisk all of your ingredients before pouring them into your prepared bowl. Cover this bowl with foil, and then pour two cups of water into your instant pot.
3. Add in your trivet, and place your bowl inside before locking the lid. Cook on high pressure for thirty minutes, and then allow for a natural pressure release before allowing it to cool for six to eight hours before serving. This gives the custard time to set.

Almond Coconut Cake

Serves: 8 **Time:** 1 Hour 10 Minutes

Calories: 231 **Protein:** 3 Grams

Fat: 19 Grams **Carbs:** 10 Grams

Ingredients:

- 1 Cup Almond Flour
- ½ Cup Coconut, Unsweetened & Shredded
- 2 Eggs, Whisked Lightly
- 1 Teaspoon Apple Pie Spice
- 1 Teaspoon Baking Powder
- 1/3 Cup Swerve
- ¼ Cup Unsalted Butter, Melted
- ½ Cup Heavy Whipping Cream

Directions:

1. Get out a round six-inch cake pan, and grease it well.

2. Take out a bowl and mix together your coconut, almond flour, swerve, apple pie spice and baking powder, making sure it's well combined. Add in your butter, cream and eggs, mixing well.

3. Pour your batter into the pan, making sure to cover it with foil.

4. Pour two cups of water into your instant pot, and then add in your trivet with the pan on top. Lock the lid, and cook on high pressure for forty minutes. Allow for a natural pressure release for ten minutes and then use a quick release to get rid of any remaining pressure.

5. Allow it to cool for at least fifteen minutes before slicing.

Chocolate Cake

Serves: 6 **Time:** 50 Minutes

Calories: 225 **Protein:** 5 Grams

Fat: 20 Grams **Carbs:** 4 Grams

Ingredients:

- 1 Cup Almond Flour
- 2/3 Cup Swerve
- ¼ Cup Cocoa Powder, Unsweetened
- ¼ Cup Walnuts, Chopped
- 1 Teaspoon Baking Powder
- 3 Eggs
- 1/3 Cup Heavy Whipping Cream
- ¼ Cup Coconut Oil

Directions:

1. Mix your cocoa powder, baking powder, swerve, flour, cream, eggs and coconut oil together, making sure it's well combined. Make sure to beat until it's fluffy.

2. Get out a heatproof pan that will fit in your instant pot, and then pour your batter into the pan before covering it with foil.

3. Pour two cups of water into your instant pot before adding in your trivet with your pan on top. Lock the lid and cook on high pressure for twenty minutes. Allow for a natural pressure release for ten minutes before using a quick release to get rid of any remaining pressure.

4. Allow it to cool for about twenty minutes before using whipped cream to top and serve.

Conclusion

Now you know everything you need to in order to get started with your instant pot! You can cook healthy low carb meals in no time at all, and the cleanup is a breeze! There's no need to worry about excessive dishes piling up or not having time to cook after work. Just pick a recipe, and find the ones you like to put together a meal plan that works for you. Healthy eating doesn't have to be hard, especially with the future of cooking now a part of your kitchen.

Made in the USA
Middletown, DE
12 November 2019